1

(PREVIEW)

"Mmmm what is it, baby? Why did you stop?" asked a confused Lia.

"I feel something hard sticking me." He said as he tried to sit up in an upright position on the sofa.

Lia groaned. "It's probably just my nipples you feel against you. They do happen to get hard like diamonds."

As enticing as Lia sounded and as bad as Derek wanted to make love to her again, he had to see what the metal object was that had stuck him on the shoulder.

Derek fished his hands around and under the side of the pillow and pulled out a watch. A watch that didn't belong to him or Lia. It was a large Rolex watch with diamonds so big it could make a blind man see. It sure as hell wasn't his.

Lia gasped as if she had seen a ghost. She brought two hands up to her face to cover up the verbal evidence that would escape from her mouth.

Reaching to turn on the lamp that sat on the end table beside the plush sofa, Derek kept his eyes glued angrily on Lia. He examined the Rolex watch; holding it up in the air as though he was investigating an object from a crime scene like Ice T did on *Law and Order.*

"Derek shook his head slowly. The frown on his forehead was cut so deep that his veins concealed through his pecan complexion. "Who does this watch belong to, Lia?"

ReNita A. Burgess's

The Belin Brothers:

A Stranger in My House

Derek

The Belin Brothers are rich, black men who are from a family of millionaires in Columbia, South Carolina. They are also successful doctors, lawyers and business owners. These brothers are smooth, classy and what every woman dreams of having. However, they each have their own drama. Secrets will be revealed as you get to know and fall in love with Calvin, Derek, Devontae, Malik and Montez.

DEDICATION AND ACKNOWLEDGMENTS

I dedicate this book to those who have had a dose of infidelity, insecurity and heartbreak. It is like being temporarily sick, but recovering from it is the best part. You are healed!

I would like to thank God, the creator and also to E. Darby for inspiring me to make my character a professional basketball coach in this book. Thanks to my editor, Lauren J, my publishing house, and to my new promoter, Kamilah Clark. (Thank you for being patient with me. I know we will be great partners.) Big shout out to all the fellow authors who are constantly grinding and working hard, you are such an inspiration to me. Thank you to my friend and best-selling author, DeMarcus James. (I know we don't talk as much anymore, but you inspire me with how quick you write and how positive you are about your talent.) I would really like to thank my family and my friends for the support most of all.

I love you!

ReNita Burgess

Xoxo

www.renitaaburgess.webs.com

Chapter 1

Her legs tightened around his waist as she straddled him in an upright position. She dipped her head back as she was taken into total ecstasy, biting her bottom lip and rolling her eyes back to her head.

Derek reached up to grab a handful of his fiancé's luscious dark hair, moaning as she took in every inch of him. She panted like a wild dog, sweat gleamed around her neck in the candle lit room.

The smell of sex and fresh laundry from the laundry room had filled their bedroom. The taste of Valentine's Day chocolate blended with their kisses as they devoured one another.

They were to remain celibate until their wedding night, but neither one of them could handle it. The urge had been out of this world, especially for Derek. He was a man, but he was a man of good moral and old fashioned respect.

"God!" He called out, squeezing her full breasts as she clenched her vaginal muscles around him. Her breast had been full as the moon that shined from their open window from the night.

"Yes, Denzel! YES!" She screamed and squirmed, wiggling through the eruption that shivered through her body.

Hold up, Derek thought. *Who the hell is Denzel and why is she calling his name instead of mine?* He stopped rocking his pelvis and looked her straight in the eyes. "Lia, you have some nerve to call another man's name in my bed, in my home! What's goin on? Who is Denzel?"

Lia shivered as she continued to release what seemed like the world's best orgasm. She ignored his question while she was trapped in a world of passion of her own. Her erect nipples pointed forward and over Derek's face. He decided to rest his hands behind his head, leaning against the headboard. *So she's going to make me wait while she gets her rocks off as I'm laying underneath her wondering who is Denzel* Derek thought as a frown curved on his forehead.

Continuing to shake from her strong collapse, Lia screamed in total desire. Whoever Denzel was sure had made her do a number on Derek. Lia was breathing heavily as she rested her head against Derek's chest. The sound of his heart beating in her ears showed that he was anxious and upset from what had just happened.

She was allowed to climax, but right there in the nick of time, his excitement was now ended. Any man would feel threatened if he heard his woman shouting out the name of another man in his home.

A devious, white smile flashed across Lia's face in the darkness of the room followed by a laugh. She was always full of surprises. The way she lured Derek with her hard to get game was what prompted him to propose to her over the year.

Confused, Derek adjusted his position to get more comfortable and study her behavior. "How are you finding this funny? We're supposed to be getting married next month and you've allowed yourself to crush me instantly by saying one word. DENZEL! Who is he?"

Lia gasped, allowing her mouth to form a round shape. "Calm down, Derek. Do you remember when your brothers and I would tease you by calling you Denzel Washington because you resembled him and recited his lines from *Training Day*?" she asked, plopping on her elbow carelessly.

The tension from Derek's face eased as the memory came to his mind. Was she saying what he thought she was saying? "I remember, but what the hell does that have to do with anything?"

She slowly started to stroke her manicured nails across the hairs on his chest as she chooses her words wisely. "Well, I .couldn't help but to remember how much you resembled Denzel Washington. I mean, you are sexy just like him. It's okay if I fantasize a little, right?"

Derek shook his head, a half smile made its way across his mouth. His chest had risen from the animosity that was living inside of him. "Do you realize how scared you had me there for a second? I wasn't sure if I was going to cry or start having a fit like Joe Jackson."

Lia pursed her lips and sat on the edge of the bed. She grabbed one of the sheets and wrapped it around her curvaceous nude body. "What grown man admits that he was going to cry?"

"A man who is in love with the woman he is about to marry." Derek leaned in to give her a kiss in which she ended shortly with a chuckle.

"Well, I'd rather have you turn into Joe Jackson. I could use a spanking every once in a while. I don't have time for a boy that wants to cry." She winked, rising to her feet.

Derek bit his lips as he slapped her on the ass, watching it jiggle underneath the satin of the wrapped sheet. "Remind me to be aggressive with you the next time then."

Lia shook her head as she started to walk towards the bathroom that was conjoined with their bedroom. Her hips swayed from side to side, reminding Derek how lucky of a man he was to have a beautiful creature such as herself. Her body could do harm by breaking necks, her eyes could hypnotize and put others under her spell just like a goddess.

Jealousy from the thought of her fantasizing about a celebrity had still triggered in his mind, even if he resembled him. His nostrils glared like a bull as he realized there was only one thing he could do to fix the situation. Derek got up from the bed and made his way into the bathroom to join his fiancé.

She looked at him confused and searched for expressions on his face. "Derek, what's the matter?"

No words came from his mouth, instead he bent her over the sink and went to work Fighting out his slight jealousy and deeply defining his infatuation for her sweetness.

He bucked and danced within her, making her grip for her life over the sink counter. He pulled her hair and bit her neck as she moaned, taking in his masculinity and introducing him to the innocent side of her. She was caught off guard and his force had been unexpected.

Derek kissed her deeply, madly and passionately. For a moment she nearly lost her balance due to the weakness and the good love making he gave her the second time around. As he walked away and left her there in the bathroom staring at him in surprise, he felt dominant. He felt as though he had conquered the jealousy he had bottled up inside of him and it was now out of his system, but he couldn't shake the fact that he felt even more curious about her ways.

Chapter 2

"Come on, bro. I know you have more spunk than that! Sock it to me!" Malik Belin said as he quickly stole the ball from Derek, pivoted on his left foot and jumped as he threw the ball into the goal. "Swoosh! That's how you do it, son!"

Derek shook his head, followed by wiping the pouring sweat from his neck. He was always the toughest one on the court, but not today. "Man, I'm only losing to you this time because I left my lucky hat. If I had worn it then I would be whipping your ass in a heartbeat. I'll always be the king."

Malik fanned him away with a laugh and rested his hands on his hips as he tried to catch his breath. "Whatever, bro. Sit down somewhere, talking about you'll always be the king. The only person I know that's the king would have to be my man, LeBron James."

"Man, LeBron wasn't the king last night. Did you catch that Cavaliers game? 3-20. LeBron was pitiful as a puppy. You may want to think twice before you bring up hot shot names like LeBron James." Derek replied.

The brothers laughed as they continued their conversation towards the parking lot. Each Sunday evening, they would meet at the court to shoot a few hopes before starting the busy work week. Their other brothers (Calvin, Montez and Devontae) would join them for a game, but everyone's schedule had been hectic over the past few weeks.

Calvin, the oldest brother and successful doctor, had recently ended a relationship with a crazy woman.

Montez, the youngest brother in medical school, was in the process of pledging a fraternity. Devontae, the nerdiest and clumsiest psychiatrist, was overwhelmed from a suicidal client he's been counseling.

Even though all the brothers were and handsome, they always made time to meet for dinner at their widowed mother's mansion in one of the wealthiest neighborhoods of Columbia, South Carolina.

"I'm going to go home and wash up before dinner, unlike some people who don't." Derek teased his brother.

Malik opened the door to his 2017 Jaguar and rested his arm on the hood before sitting down inside and starting the ignition. "Whatever, Derek. The only reason you plan to wash up is because you know that Lia won't have nothing to do with you. I still can't believe you are about to get married, bro. After all the women that we could have, you're the first one that's about to tie the knot. You do realize that's like committing suicide. You'll be with one woman for the rest of your life. That means you'll be getting the same orgasms from one woman until you're old. I doubt you'll keep getting orgasms after being with her for that long."

Derek crossed his arms over his chest with a sigh. "Well, thanks for your blessings, Malik. My apologies for not being such a hoe like you are. I take it that you're never going to settle down, right?"

"I didn't say I wasn't going to settle down. I'm just not throwing away my player's card yet. The time hasn't expired yet. I'm trying to get as much fresh kitten as I can before one woman puts a chain around my neck." Malik boasted.

His brother was always so conceited and sure of himself. It had been the nature of his ways ever since they were kids. "Okay, Malik. Maybe I've already used my player's card. Maybe I'm way ahead of you."

Shocked, Malik laughed. "Oh, okay, big brother. You are right. I can't argue with that."

"And you're supposed to be the lawyer of the family, I'm shocked." Derek told him. "I guess I won that argument and have made my point."

"Yeah, thanks for reminding me that I'll be in court each day this week. I'm trying not to think about it. Perhaps dinner at mother's tonight will help comfort me and I'll go to bed with a full stomach." Malik replied. "So is Lia coming over to join us for tonight? Or will she be missing in action again?"

Derek checked his phone to see if he had any missed calls from her. None. It wasn't like Lia. She was always known to blow his phone up and he felt he had nothing to worry about.

He always felt he had her wrapped around his finger tight, but this time he could feel her slipping for some reason. Maybe she was just as busy as she says she was, especially since she was a news photographer for the *Columbia City Times*. She had to be at every crime scene and popular event that took place in the city.

"She implied that she would be present, however I know how busy she's been with the news reporters and the detectives. Not to mention she has to be at the governor's mansion for the upcoming gala. I trust her word that she'll make it tonight, she has to. It's like ever since she's moved in with me things have been a little different." Derek said. "It could just be for the reason of us working while living together. When we weren't living together it was easier because we had to set up dates and missed each other whenever we weren't around. I guess it's natural to want to be around someone more when you don't see them every day."

Malik laughed. "Damn, man! It's gotten like that? And this is the woman you're supposed to be marrying? Well, I hope it's just because of work and nothing else If she misses dinner tonight then I would get curious."

Derek could feel the lump rising in his throat and the piercing in his heart. A part of him wished that he had never told his brother about his concern over Lia. It would only hinder his energy and stress him out even more.

He checked his watch and cleared his throat, signaling that he was ready to end the conversation. "I guess I'd better get home and take that shower. Let mother know that I'll be if you arrive early."

"Okay, brother. If you're taking the freeway, then be careful. There was an accident down that way earlier this morning." Malik replied as he adjusted the knob of his radio.

"Oh yeah? Thanks for the heads up. Are you supposed to be the angel of protection now?" Derek teased, reaching for his seat belt.

Malik gave a warm smile. "I guess you could say that. But I'm just being a concerned brother, that's all." He started his car, nodded and drove off until he made it towards the exit.

Derek was taken by surprise from his brother's sudden care for him. He knew that Malik was the ass of the family, but the guy really did care for his family. After the loss of their father dying of a heart attack, the family has been as overprotective of each other than they had ever been.

As Derek drove out of the parking lot, he noticed a few young black men walking together and sharing a few laughs.

He smiled to himself as he remembered the good ole days being a teenager, walking to the basketball court with his brothers and friends to shoot a few hoops. At that moment, he realized that life was too important to be worried.

He was already living with the woman of his dreams and would be marrying her very soon. He was sure that he was being paranoid and didn't want any fault assumptions to ruin their big plans.

Chapter 3

Derek tried his hardest to not look at the grandfather clock that stood boldly against the wall in the dining room; a tall portrait of their deceased father was right beside it. Even though their father was the one that died, he suddenly felt like he was dying the more he wondered what could be keeping Lia.

His four brothers were all present at the long dining table looking impatient as they waited on the arrival of Lia.

Shirley Belin sighed as she studied the faces of her sons and cleared her throat. "There will be no slouching at the dining table and I taught you all better than that. What if we had a very important guest here? Would you be sitting like that then?" she asked as one of the maids poured her a glass of lemonade, her favorite.

Malik, Calvin, Derek, Montez and Devontae quickly fixed their posture and directed their attention to their mother just like when they were little boys.

Their mother always knew how to set them straight and get their attention. They were all a bunch of mama's boys and she was the only woman they would allow to boss them around.

Calvin tapped his fingers against the table. "I'm ready to eat, mother. I'm starved and I had a long day at the hospital. I had to deliver two babies this morning from two different patients. Not to mention, I had no idea my schedule had gotten so full. The new receptionist forgot to block out my lunch hour so I had to work through the full day without any break."

"We've all had long days of work this week. I have one of the toughest cases in my history of being a lawyer, but you don't see me complaining like a baby, do you?" Malik said defensively, popping his collar.

Calvin rolled his eyes and started at his brother with an annoyed frown. The two of them just couldn't get along, even though they were brothers. "I was not complaining. If you didn't have your ears stuffed of ear wax, then you would have heard when I said I was ready to eat because I had a long day of work."

"Man, I don't come over here for dinner to hear you all talk about ear wax and delivering babies. I may as well leave." Devontae said, shaking his head. He knew a dinner table brawl was about to take place between Calvin and Malik as always.

Montez, the youngest brother, sighed as he began devouring his meal. "Well, I'm going to go ahead and get started eating. Lia is late and doesn't seem to be joining us for dinner Meanwhile, it's going to be a long night since Dumb Ass #1 and Dumb Ass #2 are arguing like two old men."

Shirley stood to her feet slowly, being cautious because of her arthritis and stiff joints. Even though she was elderly, she always made sure she looked as good as her money. "Boys, you are all making this dinner a disaster. Calvin and Malik are arguing, Montez has started his dinner before saying grace, Devontae is getting disgusted from hearing the complaints and Derek's fiancé has stood us up once again for Sunday dinner. Had she been here as planned then this outburst wouldn't have occurred."

"Mother, do you mind passing the salt? This yellow rice needs a little more taste for flavor." Montez asked with a mouth full of food.

Shirley couldn't believe it as she slapped her son on the head with her coin purse. The rest of the brothers laughed, which seemed to lower all the uproar that was going on.

"What? Why did you have to do that? I just recently had my dreadlocks re-twisted." Said a surprised Montez.

"Because I am trying to show all of you how you are behaving. I didn't raise my sons to behave like The Beverly Hillbillies or Duck Dynasty just so they could live in this mansion and go to the finest schools. Compose yourselves!" Shirley snapped.

The brothers all cleared their throats and did as their mother instructed. When it came to demands and getting a point across, their mother knew how to put them in place.

Shirley took a seat and observed her glare around the table at her sons. "Now let's all say grace and go on with our family meal. Bow your heads."

All their heads were bowed as they prepared to eat the fine meal that was prepared for them. Derek looked up at the clock, noticing that the long hand had finally hit the four. It was now 7:20 and he knew that Lia would be skipping another dinner with he and his family.

As his head was bowed, he felt his cellular phone vibrating in the pocket of his slacks. He carefully pulled it out and slid his thumb across the screen. His heart sunk in his chest as he read the text that Lia had sent.

"Hey, babe. Don't kill me, but I'm not going to be able to make it to dinner with you all tonight. Looks like it's another long night of editing these photos in the office. It seems we have to print the article of the oldest woman living in South Carolina by this Tuesday. Don't wait up for me. Sending everyone my love. Lia.

Shaking his head in disbelief and sucking his teeth, Derek just couldn't believe that Lia was making this into a repeated pattern. *Was she really working late?* He thought.

"Derek, we are trying to say grace and you're looking around like you're lost. Bow your head and don't be disrespectful." Shirley interrupted

Derek snapped out of it. "I'm sorry, mother. I just have a few things on my mind. I'm sorry."

"Don't say sorry, say I apologize. Sorry is for weak minded boys and I didn't raise boys in this Belin generation. I raised men Now bow your head and let me continue with saying grace." Shirley replied.

"Yes, mother." Derek obeyed. But before he bowed his head, he looked over at Malik who had shook his head. He knew that Derek was disappointed about Lia's sudden whereabouts. The sun was setting through the nearby window and the shadows of the trees hid behind the curtains. What hid in the dark would soon come out in the light.

Chapter 4

"You all know how tough the Florida Fins are. If it hadn't been for them winning us, our team would have been undefeated and we would have made it to the playoffs. I hope that you all have learned your lesson and plan to kick their asses this year." Derek said as he paced back and forth beside the edge of the gym floor.

A wooden clipboard rested under his armpit as he tucked his hands into the pockets of his relaxed khaki pants. He fanned away a fly that had been flying around the collar of his royal purple J. Crew shirt.

All fifteen of the athletes sat attentively on the bleachers, their faces drenched in sweat from the long day of practice they had endured.

"With all due respect, Coach Belin. We would have won that game had it not been for Pierce over there showing off his fancy moves on the court instead of passing the ball or making a throw." Tyron Lewis chimed in. He was one of the point guards and he took his career as a professional basketball player very serious.

Phillip Pierce stood to his feet and boastfully walked over to TyRon like a lion inspecting his prey. Both of the athletes stood around seven feet tall and when they were face it face, they looked like the twin towers at the World Trade Center.

Derek shook his head with a sigh for he knew that war was about to break loose between the two young men.

"Don't worry about what I'm doing on that court, TyRon. The only thing that you should be worried about is keeping that damn seat warm on the bleachers like you always do." Phillip snapped back at him.

The other basketball players laughed, pushing up the animosity of the bitter team mates.

"Okay, so it's like that, huh? I'll tell you what. If you don't take your Kunta Kinte ass back over there then I'm going to do-"

Derek stood between the men so that they weren't standing so close enough to harm each other. His hands pushed them both away as he blew the whistle in his mouth. "You're going do nothing, TyRon. Both of you go back and take a seat. We're still in the middle of a basketball meeting here."

"Yes, sir." They both said, aggravated.

The assistant coach, Coach Andrew Myers, had walked over to Derek and let him know that Lia had called him from the office.

Derek excused himself as he walked through the exit towards his office. A janitor nodded his head at him as he mopped along the floors and continued to do his work.

The office was much cooler inside than the other parts of the building. Photos of him and Lia were on his desk and a few hung against the wall beside his South Carolina University Master's Degree in Health Science.

Derek cleared his throat before he placed the phone to his ear to hear the reason for his fiancé calling him. "Hello?"

"Derek, baby, when are you coming home? I'm lonely and I need to know when to start dinner." Lia pouted.

This came as a surprise to him because for the past few weeks she had been busy and somewhat distant towards him. "Oh, is that so? I'm at a loss for words."

Lia laughed. "Why is that, baby? Is it because I've been so tired lately and tied up in my work?"

Not wanting to sound like he was sweating her, Derek kept his cool like any man would. "Actually, I assumed you would be busy, being that you missed dinner with my family on numerous occasions."

"Oh, so are you keeping count? Well, excuse me for being passionate about my work." Lia said, anger rising in her voice.

Derek sighed. He really wasn't in the mood to argue with his soon to be wife before they tied the knot. "Baby, I'm sorry. It's just that I hardly see you as much even though we are living together. The only time we see each other is when we get ready for bed. I had no idea your job as a photographer is busier than my job as a professional basketball coach."

"What is that supposed to mean, Derek? Are you trying to say that my job isn't as important as yours just because you coach a very popular basketball team and have meetings with ESPN?" Lia snapped.

"Sweetheart, I may be busy in and out of meetings, but at least at the end of the day I try to make time for the person I choose to marry which is far more important." Derek explained. He felt like he had been waiting forever to point that out to her. For some reason, he felt relieved. However, Lia wasn't going to be the one with a sense of relief.

The other line of the phone was silent for a few moments.

"Lia, are you there? Hello?"

Click.

Damn. The only thing Derek could hear on the other line was the sound of the busy tone, leaving him aware that she had hung up on him.

That was cold.

Derek slowly placed the phone back down on the receiver and looked around his office and up at the ceiling as though he wanted an answer from God.

He was interrupted by a knock on the door. Derek led his attention to see one of his best players standing there, waiting for him.

"Coach Belin, I'm sorry to intrude on you like this, but Coach Myers says that we need to wrap things up. Should I tell him you'll be out shortly?" asked Brian.

Derek ran both hands over his forehead and took a deep breath as if he had a headache. "It's cool, brother. I'm coming out right now. I'm sorry for the lengthy phone call I had with my fiancé."

Brian laughed as he patted Derek on the back. "Man, I understand. I know how women are these days. You can't live with them and can't live without them. If you ever need to talk man to man, then I'm here."

Hearing that statement come from a much younger man had surely done him all the good to uplift his energy, especially after his little quarrel with Lia. "Thanks for the lecture, young man. How old are you again? Twenty? Nineteen? Don't you still have your mother's breast milk around your mouth?"

"Coach Belin, I may be young, but I sure do know about women. Probably more than you will ever know. You just have to know how to get under their skin and confuse them up a little, they'll be like a puppet and all you have to do is just pull the string, my man." Brian added.

Derek laughed again, this time much louder as they headed towards the exit towards the opening of the gym. He gave Brian a pat on the back. "Kid, you're a case."

As they made their way to gather with the other players, Derek noticed they were all laughing with each other and sharing a few jokes.

A few of them were even shooting some hoops as they waited on Derek to return. That's one thing he loved about being their coach, they always waited on him and listened to him loyally, unlike Lia who had been difficult for the past few weeks. He just assumed that she was getting pre-wedding jitters.

"Hey, coach. We just came up with a good idea for our game plan. What do you think about-"

One of the athletes was interrupted when the side door to the arena opened and realized what appeared to be a woman entering. Wolf whistles started to echo across the gym as Lia stood under the exit sign, tilting her Louis Vuitton shades to her forehead as though she was a movie star.

Every curve of her booty moved with grace as her breasts bounced in the low v-cut blouse she wore. Her ass jiggled into motion through the thin white pants she wore. The athletes stared and gave her their attention as she made her way towards their hurdle.

"Man, you are one lucky, brotha. I'll give ya that." Coach Myers said as he gave Derek a hand slap.

Even though there was a frown on Derek's forehead, a smile formed across his face. How could he stay mad at the woman? But what he was curious about was why was she there at his place of work?

What in the hell did she wanted for her to not wait until they had some privacy alone to discuss? Derek didn't know, but he was about to find out.

The wolf whistles and cat hisses grew even more as Lia continued to walk towards them. Lia could feel the confidence arising in her with every step.

She switched her big hips a little more, getting into the feel of being admired by the many men in the building. Somehow she got a little too carried away when she fell to the floor in her Jimmy Choo heels.

Everyone rushed to her aid to see if she was okay, but from the look of things, she seemed to be in agony as she held on to her ankle. Derek pushed everyone out the way as he took over to be at his fiancé's side. Even though she had sprained her ankle, it was a serious matter to him. He loved Lia with every ounce of emotion in his beating heart and he wanted to be there for her through everything.

He didn't want to waste his time having arguments with her before they tied the knot. Maybe her minor injury would make her forget about their little mishap they experienced earlier. He kept his hopes high that the incident would only bring them closer together, to show her how much he needed and wanted to love her. Or could it bring out the worse in things?

Chapter 5

Lia cried in pain as she held on tightly to her ankle. Even when she tried to move she was unsuccessful.

"We may need to call the paramedics. She could have pulled a muscle." Said Coach Myers, wiping the sweat away from his forehead.

Derek and one of the athletes tried to help her get to her feet. "Easy...easy." Derek said. "Do you feel you need a paramedic, Lia?"

Lia closed her eyes as she fought through the pain. "I'm okay. I don't need a paramedic. It's not like I'm dying." She snapped.

A few of the other athletes started to laugh at the way she used sarcasm against him.

Derek struggled to assist her with getting up, but she was reluctant to his help. She was too bold, too stubborn and too independent.

"Baby, if you just stop acting like super woman and let me take care of you then maybe you won't put your ankle in more pain. What's your problem, woman?" Derek remarked.

Rolling her eyes and shaking her head, Lia took a deep breath. "That's the problem with you, men. So many of you think that just because we're a woman that we're weak and always need the help from a man."

The rest of the men were all drawn into their dramatic scene, in a way which seemed cute and romantic.

"I guess you're only not trying to be super woman, but you're also trying to be a feminist." Derek decided to pick her up in his arms gently, as though he was holding a baby. The upper body training he did on a regular basis in the gym had definitely paid off. The way he carried Lia showed that he was a provider and a really strong man.

"Put me down! Put me down, Derek Belin!" she shouted.

"Well, you may as well get used to me carrying you because this is how I will be carrying you over the threshold." He laughed.

The rest of the crew continued to be amused in laughter, cheering them on. Lia realized that she couldn't stay upset at Derek for much longer. After all, the man was carrying her like a princess and treating her like a queen. "Derek, how in the hell do you put up with me?" she asked.

Derek kissed her on the forehead. "I put up with you because I love you and it comes with the package. If you're being bitchy then that's just something I'll have to put up with."

Lia gasped and gave him a playful laugh. "You take that back, Derek Belin."

Applauds filled the gymnasium as Derek told the teammates and Coach Myers goodbye for the evening. He carried his wife to be to his car, opening the car door at the same time.

"Derek, if you drop me with this injured ankle then I swear I will slap you again and this time it won't be playful." She assured him as she pursed her lips.

Derek gently placed her into the passenger's seat, a sly smile spread across his lips. "You're supposed to trust me, babe." He said, patting his pants pockets as though he had forgotten something.

Lia bit down on her bottom lip as she looked up at Derek, confused. "Did you forget something, sweetheart?"

"Umm yeah. As a matter of fact, I did. I left my car keys on the fold out table inside the gymnasium. I'll be right back. Don't you go anywhere, baby?" Derek pointed a finger.

Rolling her eyes followed by a sigh, Lia laughed. "How can I? I can barely walk on this foot. Nice joke."

As Derek headed towards the doors of the gymnasium, he ran a little just to speed up his pace. He quickly checked his watch and walked inside. Some of the basketball players were still talking and a few of them were heading towards the exit door to leave for the rest of the evening.

"Hey, coach. Are you looking for these?" asked Jamal, holding the pair of shiny keys in the air.

From where Derek was standing, the keys being held in the air so high from a guy that stood seven-foot-tall made him feel like he was looking up towards a mountain.

Derek smiled, relieved. "You have my keys. Phew. Thanks for looking out, brah. I was starting to freak out and believing that someone would steal them."

Jamal placed a hand on his hips. The reflection from the light was shining down on the top of his bald head. "Coach, why would you say that? What, you don't trust your players? What kind of sportsmanship is that?" he teased.

"Nah, that's not what I'm saying, son. I just thought that by the time I got here that-"

"That one of us would have stolen your ole keys." Jamal finished Derek's sentence for him. He raised his voice to catch the attention of his teammates. "Hey, yo! Coach Belin over here forgot his keys and rushed back inside to get them because he thought that one of us would have stolen them!"

Derek laughed, realizing that Jamal was always full of jokes. The rest of the team started charging up on Derek and roughing him up. Derek tried to reach for the keys as Jamal taunted him,

45

holding them higher in the air. Laughter was endless as Derek jumped using all his might just to grab the keys.

"Come on, man. Stop playing like that. I'm your coach." Pleaded a breathless Derek. "I have my fiancé sitting in the car waiting for me to take her home."

"Coach Belin, you're out of breath. I guess because you're getting old or just getting out of shape." Laughed one of the teammates.

"That's a good one, Kendrick." Laughed another.

"Stop horsing around, Jamal and hand over my damn keys. I really need to get the hell out of here." Derek demanded. He was much serious this time and started to worry about Lia sitting outside in the car.

Everyone booed him as Jamal gave him the keys. "Here you go, coach. Lighten up and have a good laugh every now and then. We have a big game coming up and it's doing us all the good to make fun of you."

Derek shook his head. "Yeah, whatever. I'm glad to see that you guys are using me as your source of entertainment. Why not let me fill out an application for a career as a clown instead of a coach?"

They all laughed and patted him on the back as he continued towards the exit. Derek loved his basketball players, but sometimes they were a little too childish for their ages. He figured that with all the pressure they were under as professional athletes, perhaps they needed to be amused every chance they got.

The chill of the air had hit against Derek's face once he had stepped foot outside. The trees swayed with the wind as leaves fell gracefully to the ground.

At that moment, Derek gasped from the scene that took place from his car. What in the hell was Lia doing and why was she laughing so much with one of the basketball players? A frown carved its way in the middle of Derek's forehead. *Oh, some shit is about to go down and he was about to find out.*

Chapter 6

"What's going on? Is everything alright?" Derek asked, waiting for an answer. Lia seemed shocked as she looked up at Derek. Derek couldn't help but to wonder the sudden look of shock on her face.

"Hi Coach Belin. I was trying to catch up with you to give you the keys you left in your office." The basketball player said.

Derek stood frozen. His brown gaze pierced through the young man as he wondered what was he doing in his office. As a matter of fact, he wasn't even sure who this athlete was and didn't remember putting him on the team. He had seen him before, but the guy was always quiet.

He couldn't even recall his name. He wasn't as tall as the other basketball players, he probably stood around 5'10 and his body frame was thin and lanky. He wore a baseball cap over his trimmed haircut, the diamond stud in his right ear gave a certain glow to his light brown skin.

He probably didn't know this guy too well for the fact that he may have always sat on the bench during the games, that could be a really good reason.

Lia swallowed and stretched her eyes as she tried to fill in the answers. "Denzel says that Coach Myers asked him to turn off the light that you left on in your office. Honey, what did I tell you about wasting electricity? You do it all the time at home."

Denzel laughed at Lia's remark. The only person who wasn't laughing along with them was Derek, of course. He found no sense in this funny as he studied both of them, left and right. Derek folded his arms across his chest before he took the keys carefully from Denzel's hand.

"Honey, lighten up and take a joke. You were just joking around with me in there when I refused to be carried." Lia smirked.

"The joke isn't what I'm concerned about, Lia. I would like to know why would Coach Myers send someone in my office without my consent?" asked Derek, keeping his eyes on Denzel.

"Well, baby. It's because he thought you were already gone out the building. Nobody wants to leave the light on in the building and run up the electric build." Lia said as she shrugged her shoulders.

Derek rolled his eyes, his nose glared. "You know damn well this stadium is owned by billionaire's and that I'm a part of the organization. Stop giving me the lame excuses. The electrical bill is never going to be an issue, Lia."

Lia rested her head back on the seat. "Baby let's just go home and spend that time together that you wanted to spend with me."

"Oh, so you're making it seem like you're taking time out of your busy schedule to make time for me. Is that what it is, Lia? You should be wanting to spend time with me on your own. It shouldn't be like you're spending time with me just because I wanted to. It doesn't work that way." Derek said. He tried his best to control his temper. His mother had always told his brothers not to tease him too much or he would flip out on them unexpectedly.

Denzel was about to walk away

Derek looked up and down at Denzel as though he was a piece of meat. "Wait…did you just say his name was Denzel?"

There was silence for a moment between the three of them. It had all made sense when Derek realized that Denzel was the name she was screaming out during their heated sexual performance the other night.

Lia remembered playing it off and telling Derek her reason for calling out the name Denzel and her excuse was that Derek resembled the actor Denzel Washington. Derek wasn't stupid. For some reason he had a disturbing hunch that Denzel was the guy standing in front of him.

"Is your name Denzel? I don't recall you ever informing me that your name was Denzel when you were recruited to the team." Derek asked sternly, tapping his fingers on the roof of his car as he impatiently waited for an answer.

Biting her bottom lip, Lia spoke quickly. "Uhh, baby. Denzel is Eric's middle name."

Now this shit was starting to become an unsolved mystery. Why was she calling him by his middle name and not by his first name? It seemed to him like she had already knew him personally. Suddenly, he remembered the guy's name was Eric. Eric Bradley.

Eric was a new team member who had been recruited over from the San Antonia Steamers earlier in the year. He used to always wear those huge glasses like Dwayne Wade in the beginning, making it hard for anyone to notice him.

This time he had his glasses off and that was why Derek hadn't recognize him. The kid was like a ghost anyhow because he spent most of his time sitting on the bench during a game.

"Look, Coach Belin. I don't want to intrude or cause any dilemmas between you and Lia, but.."

Derek interrupted Eric once again, using his hands to gesture the time-out sign. "Wait. How did you know her name was Lia? This is her first time coming here during practice." Derek guarded his gaze towards Lia and then back at Eric.

Eric gulped, the look of fear was on his face and he was starting to look like a little boy who was caught with his hands in the cookie jar.

Lia was about to speak, but Derek cut her off. "Let the boy speak, Lia. You've done enough talking already."

Eric was caught off guard when Derek referred to him as a boy. The frown that appeared in the middle of his forehead showed that he felt belittled and offended.

"Like I said, coach Belin. I don't want to cause any trouble. I was just speaking with your fiancé and."

"Brother, you may as well refer to her as Lia since the cat's already out of the bag." Derek replied.

"Derek, calm down! What's wrong with you?" Lia demanded.

This time Eric felt this was being taken too far. He stormed away with anger in his eyes, he didn't even bother to look over his shoulder at Derek and Lia.

Derek shook his head as he walked over to the driver's side of his car. After he had got in, he slammed his door shut and cranked up the door, storming off past Eric who was still walking. Lia's head jerked as she held on to the inside door handle.

She had never seen Derek with such outrage before, but for some reason it had turned her on. Lia knew that when they got home, she would have a whole lot of explaining to do.

She looked over at Derek who had been driving like he was on a road rampage. They rode in silence as he kept his eyes fixed on the road, going past the speed limit.

Chapter 7

"How the fuck did he know that your name, Lia? You never…come out to the practice to meet any…of…mmmm..of the athletes?" Derek asked as he roared his pelvis into a moaning Lia.

Her eyes rolled to the back of her head as he rammed in between the slippery wetness of her legs. The look on her face was one that showed possession. She bit her bottom lip as she sunk her nails into the muscles of his broad back.

"I….mmmmmm…. I….I told him….that I was your…fiancé…when …he asked where you were…Ohhhhhhh shit, baby!!! That shit feels so good!!!!" Lia moaned into his ear.

Derek decided to tantalize her clit by hitting the head of his hardened shift against it. He teased her until she forced him inside of her deeper, finding her pleasure zone from many different angles.

"I'll teach you not to flirt with guys anymore. Was that the guy's name you were calling out the other night?" Derek rammed harder.

Lia's mouth was opened as wide as possible. She was still recovering from one of her intense orgasms.

"Answer me, Lia!" Derek pumped harder, relieving his frustration into her with both pleasure and pain.

"Baby, mmmm no. I wasn't...calling his ...name out. It was a coincidence. Mmmmm please don't stop." Lia squealed.

Derek wanted to stop to make her suffer from the power of his magical manhood, but their makeup sex was on point and probably one of the best sexual performed they have ever endured.

He didn't stop. He couldn't stop. He kept on going. He pulled up one of her legs and tossed it over his shoulder for deeper penetration.

Once he had her where he wanted, he used his hard work in the perfect angle. He forced his large member into her, hoping to leave her sore from his control.

Lia grabbed his ass, pinning him through her. She smiled as she felt his collapsing into her anatomy. He poured and she splashed, together they released the most outstanding waterfall that human nature could create.

Derek rested his head on Lia's chest, both of their bodies were drenched in cold sweat as their lethargic breathing cooled them off.

Lia ran her hands through Derek's damp hair as he sighed among her breasts. "Baby, I've never seen you this aggressive during sex before. Mmmm maybe I should make you upset at me more often."

Looking up into Lia's eyes, Derek couldn't deny that he loved the woman, even through the times that he hated her.

"I had a lot of frustration bottled up inside, Lia. What was I supposed to do?" he asked with a tired smile.

Lia stroked his facial hair and pinched his nose. "Well, you could give me a heads up the next time you plan to pierce through me. I may have to end up getting vaginal rejuvenation because of your ass."

Derek kissed her on the forehead and rolled over until he was off the bed and on to his feet. "You know how us Belin men are. We're demanding and controlling at times. We like to have our way." He looked over his shoulder at her with a wink.

Pulling the white satin sheets up to her face to cover her smile and nude body, she giggled like a little girl.

Derek loved the outline of her curvaceous body concealing through the sheet. The way she smiled would always send shivers up and down his spine. He walked over to her, leaning over to kiss her on her soft, sensuous lips. The taste of cherry flavored lip gloss left its mark on his taste buds. Derek couldn't wait to make every part of her his forever. Hopefully, she was telling the truth about not being unfaithful with someone named Denzel.

He could only hope, wish and pray that it was coincidental. The rough love making was enough to make any woman spill the truth, but how could she tell the truth through all the intense pleasure?

Even if she wasn't telling the truth, at least the joy from his magic stick would make her not want to drift away to another man. He smiled as he had flashbacks of her gripping on to the sheets, biting her lips and rolling her eyes to the back of her head. He knew he had a good woman. He just had to get over his assumptions before they created any chaos and havoc. *Fan the flames* he thought to himself, *just fan the flames.*

****

Derek, Devontae, Calvin, Malik and Montez all decided to watch the basketball game in the V.I.P room of the night club that Derek owned and managed. It was one of the most popular clubs in downtown Columbia. Whenever the celebrities would come into town, his club was the top place of attraction.

The upscale style night club had a neon colored spiral upstairs leading up to the second floor made of glass in which you could see the guest dancing or having drinks at the glow in the dark bar.

The upstairs portion was classier than the raunchy portion downstairs. Derek enjoyed the feeling of having what seemed like two clubs in one. The music and the food was always the best quality and the atmosphere was always fun.

"Yo, did you see that pass that Jamal Kimble just gave? He wasn't even trying to pay attention to the point guard." Malik said eagerly, gulping down a shot of vodka.

All five of the brothers jumped from their seats as they made loud noises in an outburst in reaction to the basketball game.

"That shot was sweeeeeet!" shouted Devontae, slapping his hand on the round table.

"Looks like the Mustangs are going to win this one tonight. I had better call up my homeboys and ask them when will they be paying me." Calvin laughed as he started to stroll through the contacts of his cell phone.

A drunken Montez slapped his brother on the back. "Calvin, they still have to do a free throw. Don't get your hopes up, man."

"I'm not getting my hopes up." Calvin said. "I'm just speaking it into existence."

The five of them all shared a few laughs as they waited for the commercials to be over with.

Malik was standing under the flat screen television set on wall as he waited anxiously for the game to come back on. "Do you all know that I have a court trial for Anthony Peters next week? You know, Anthony Peters of the Minnesota Wolves."

They all gave him their attention in total astonishment.

"Why the hell is he going to court?" Derek asked.

"Yeah, don't tell me he's on drugs or something. He is always looking as if he's on drugs or pissy drunk when he's on the basketball court. That could be the reason why their team is suffering from so many losses this year." Montez said, shaking his head.

Devontae rolled his eyes. "Tez, you have no room to talk because you are drunk as a skunk right now."

"Being drunk isn't the same as being high on drugs. And besides, it's appropriate for me to get drunk every blue moon. I'm a student in medical school and I need as much relief as I can get. Plenty of sex and plenty of alcohol from time to time won't hurt no body." Montez chuckled, taking a swig of his alcoholic beverage.

"Wait, will you guys just stop trying to guess while he's going to trial and let me tell you why?" Malik motioned with his hands until his brothers became silent to hear what he had to say. "Okay, thank you." He cleared his throat. "It appears that my client Anthony Peters, will be in court next week for domestic violence against his wife."

Calvin gasped. "Damn, why was he fighting his wife? What did she do?"

"It's a damn shame that some men will stoop as low just to hit a woman. I'm glad our parents taught us right from wrong. This dude has everything money can buy and he's giving his life away by beating up on a woman like some punk." Devontae said, rubbing his forehead.

"Yeah, man, but you don't know why Anthony was causing this physical abuse towards her. See, let me tell ya'll what's up." Malik cleared his throat again. "She was cheating on him with his bodyguard. Ain't that some twisted shit? You can't trust women these days."

"It doesn't surprise me not a damn bit why she would cheat. Anthony had so many female fans around him every minute. Don't tell me a man isn't going to get tempted when he's on the road playing basketball. He was seeing beautiful pussy on a regular basis." Montez shock his dreadlocks from his face.

Derek could feel his face getting hot as he felt his own insecurity rise from his thoughts of Lia. He started to wonder again if she was referring to Eric's middle name, Denzel or Denzel Washington the actor. Derek's palms started to sweat as the thoughts of Lia laughing with Eric in the parking lot.

What if he would soon be in the same situation as the famous basketball star, Anthony Peters? Nah, he couldn't see himself physically abusing Lia if she had cheated on him like that. He realized that if that ever happened to him, he wasn't sure what he would do.

He would be so hurt that he probably wouldn't be able to think clearly. He truly loved Lia and didn't even want to think of the thought of losing her to someone else. He scratched his head as the pellets of warm sweat formed around his mustache.

"Could we just change the subject from discussing a man's personal life?" Derek asked, looking up at the television as the basketball game returned from the lengthy commercials.

Calvin rubbed hands together. "Why are you being so defensive, brother?"

"Nothing, man. I just don't think it's fair that we talk about this like some gossiping hood-rats at a ghetto beauty salon." Derek replied carelessly as his heart was beating heavy like loud drums. He didn't want all of his brothers to become curious of his curiosity.

They were quiet for a moment, savoring in the awkwardness before getting back in tune with the game. Beautiful women underneath them downstairs were entering the club wearing close to nothing in miniskirts and high heels. Malik had to excuse himself as he allowed his second head to lead the way in that direction.

"You all will have to let me know who won the game. I have to go mingle because I'm single." Malik laughed while rushing downstairs to the main floor.

"One day somebody is gonna beat him at his own game and play him like the women he plays." Devontae said, keeping his eyes glued to the television.

"Are you okay, Derek?" Calvin asked with concern in his voice.

Derek gulped. Dammit. He didn't want anyone else to assume that he was having personal problems in his relationship. It would be an embarrassment, especially since he was engaged to the woman and not even married to her yet. "Me? I'm fine. I just don't like hearing about adultery when I'm going to be getting hitched very soon. You know how that goes?"

"Hey, I understand, man. I don't know what Malik was thinking. He's always the dramatic one, but I'm sure he meant no harm and forgot that it seemed rude to bring up a topic like that since we've always been single."

Shaking his head in agreement, Derek had to admit that his big brother was right. "True. You have a point there, Calvin."

"SLAM DUNK! DID YOU SEE THAT MOVE BY KADEEM MOORE? THAT BROTHER IS ON FIRE TONIGHT!!!" Montez shouted while excitedly clapping his hands.

Just as Derek was getting back into the game, his phone was ringing and someone was calling from a blocked number. He motioned his expression curiously as he dipped his head back to view the private listing on his phone.

"Hello?" he answered.

There was no respond; only heavy breathing through the receiver.

"Hello?" Derek answered again.

More heavy breathing.

(Click)

That was rather strange and unusual for someone to call his phone and not say anything. For a moment he wondered if it was Lia calling to play a trick on him because she was at home alone with a broken foot, but he realized that she went to bed early before he left out the house; or wasn't she?

The phone was ringing again and this time Derek answered it with aggravation in his voice versus the pleasant tone he offered previously. Whoever this person was they were playing games and it was starting to piss him off as much as generic toilet paper.

"HELLO??!!" He shouted, causing Montez, Calvin and Devontae to stop and stare.

What Derek had heard from the other end of his phone was enough to make a man want to cry. He heard what he thought were sounds of sex coming from the background of a porno movie, but as he listened in closely the sexual moaning sounded familiar.

The sound of sweet ecstasy being played to his ear sounded like they were coming from Lia, his own fiancé. Who would want to play this trick on him and why would Lia allow this happen? So much was running through his mind at the moment as his blood boiled. He felt his eyes stinging from the tears that were struggling to come down.

Whoever the person was on the other line decided to bring in the phone louder so that he could hear the sound of the bed squeaking as the sexual moans increased.

That was that and enough was enough! He ended the call, grabbed his Burberry Gabardine trench coat and stormed out the door fast as lightening. At that point, he wasn't sure what he was going to do. Perhaps he could clearly understand why Anthony Peters was going to be charged with domestic violence.

Chapter 8

Storming through the city traffic, Derek couldn't wait for the stop light to turn green. He needed to immediately go to his two story house to find out who was there and who was making his fiancé scream louder sexually than he did.

Passengers honked the horn of their vehicles at him as the others shouted obscene profanity. He could care less what they thought or what they were saying.

All he cared about was getting to home, rushing up the stairs to see what was going on. The first thing he wanted to do was bash in the skull of the man that was making love to his woman.

Even though his mother taught him never to hit a woman or harm her in any way, the second thing he wanted to do was slap the living hell and daylights out of Lia.

His foot added more pressure to the pedal, allowing the speedometer to go to 95 miles per hour. "That BITCH! That BITCH!" was all he could say. How could she betray him this way?

another man to screw her over the phone and in his ears. Oh, he couldn't wait to get his hands on both of them. Derek was even shocked in himself. Never had he had this type of

Derek pulled his black Mustang into their enormous sized yard, flying into the driveway like an escaped bat from hell. Their yard was half as big as a football field, but it was surrounded with neatly trimmed hedges and a picket fence that made everything seem perfect.

He wasted no time in waiting to stop his car before opening the door and then slamming it. Derek anxiously ran up the stairs of the porch and fumbled his fingers through the keys nervously.

The door slammed against the wall, causing a portrait of him and Lia to fall to the floor; leaving shards of glass everywhere. Derek paid it no mind as he looked around his home. He could tell that someone was there.

He could smell the cologne of another man mixed with the scent of sex in the atmosphere. Soft jazz was playing on the radio in the English style kitchen from a distance.

Derek heard some stomps and a gasp coming from upstairs. He ran up the stairs like those FBI cops did whenever they were about to raid a crack house.

He stood in front of the bedroom door shaking his head and biting his lips. He made a tight fist, so tight that his nails dug into the palm of his hand causing pain to rise though him. As he placed his ear to the door, he heard footsteps.

"Lia! Lia, open up? Who is in there with you, huh? I'm not playing any games? Was it Denzel?!! Open up!" He shouted. "If you don't open up then I'm gonna knock the door down! I'm not playing!"

There was silence for a moment. She wasn't responding but the door was locked. She had to be in there. Either she was in there or she was trying to hide the evidence of another man.

"LIA!"

Okay, that was it. Derek was about to tear down the bedroom door of their mansion. He made enough money to have it repaired again and that was the least of his problems.

Derek stepped back like a raging bull preparing to run through a red cape. He used his shoulders to give the door at least four hard blows and that's when he heard a scream.

"Derek! What are you doing?" Lia screamed. It was then that the lock on the door was already ripped apart, Lia was sitting up in the bed with the covers over her face.

"Why the hell is someone calling my phone and letting me listen in on you being fucked by them?!?" Derek shouted, standing over her.

Her body was shaking like a limb on a tree and her lips quivered as though she was freezing.

The color in her face went from a soft brown to a dark blue, sweat pellets formed around the temples of her forehead. "Derek, baby! What are you talking about? Please, calm down! Obviously someone must be playing a trick on you or something. You know damn well that you have people out there jealous of you for your career and the fact that you come from a wealthy family. Maybe it was that guy we were talking to yesterday in the parking lot. You know, one of the basketball players. The one named Eric or Denzel!"

Shaking his head and catching up with her game, Derek wasn't about to fall for it this time. He paced back and forth around the bed. "Oh, you mean the one that YOU were talking to yesterday! I know he's an alternative player on my team, but I don't know him like that. You seemed to know him well and now you're acting totally clueless about him. You're full of games, Lia! You're cheating on me with some young dick or not?! Just let me know so I can take back the engagement ring and move the hell on with my fuckin life!!"

Lia wiped the tears away from her eyes quickly. "How in the hell could I cheat on you or have someone in here when I can barely walk after spraining my ankle? You would really think I would stoop that low to do that with an injury? Do you think I'm that desperate, Derek? You know, I think you're just trying to come up with an excuse not to marry me and trying to turn the tables around.

Maybe you're just imagining things! You ever thought of that?"

Not knowing what to believe, all Derek could do was walk back over to Lia and embrace her. He held her as a small tear drop fell from his cheek. He was a strong man, but he was also a weak man when it came to love. He cradled Lia's beautiful face in the cup of his hands.

"Baby, I just don't want you out of my life. I love you so much that it kills me to think that you're sleeping behind my back with another man. The thought of it just tortures me. I freak out, but I'm so confused." Derek said softly.

Lia smiled, kissing him on the cheek. "It's okay, honey. You're just worried because we'll be married and you don't want to be hurt during the marriage. It's normal for all engaged couples to behave this way, to feel like something is happening or going to happen." She stood to her feet painfully as she got up from the bed.

The negligee she wore clanged to her hourglass figure, her cleavage popped out like two full moons side by side. She was just too beautiful to turn away from.

Even if she had been cheating, Derek knew it would be hard to get over her or to end their relationship. He always thought of how beautiful their kids would turn out and he didn't want to miss that chance.

Maybe she was right, maybe it was someone playing tricks on him. Malik was the only one that knew he was having problems with Lia being distant. After all, Eric could even be behind it as well. Maybe it wasn't Eric or Malik at all. It could just be Lia playing around with him all along.

There was still so much explaining to do; like why did the sexually moaning woman over the phone sounded so much like Lia? Why did the house smell like unfamiliar strong male cologne?

Why did it feel like someone had been there and then left right before he came in? And most of all, why was Lia limping on the opposite feet than the one that was injured?

Whatever it was or whatever was going on, Derek knew he would get to the bottom of it. His mind was too disheveled and all over the place as he thought of everything.

It just didn't make any sense. He shook his head as he watched her standing in front of their full length mirror to comb her hair. If she was lying, then she sure was a damn good liar.

Chapter 9

The score on the board was 28-30 and they were in the last quarter of the game. ESPN reporters stood on the sidelines in front of cameras and the cheerleaders expressed their enthusiastic spirit.

The referee blew his whistle and signaled that Georgia Mountain Lions tossed a foul ball. The coaches paced back and forth nervously, keeping their eyes fixated on the basketball being tossed from player to player.

Derek wiped the sweat away from his forehead and Coach Myers clapped his hands as he shouted at their team. "Come on guys, stay in there! Stay in there! Just get this last shot and we are in, baby!!!"

Grady O'Kendal stole the ball from a Lions defense point guard. He was one of the shortest players on the team but he was fast as lightening. He passed the ball to the shooting guard, Chico Laney.

Chico stood around 6 ft. 6 and he was one of the reasons that the Carolina Stingers was one of the best teams in the Professional Basketball Association. He didn't even have to jump really high to make the basketball go in the goal. It was never a struggle for him and it was always a piece of cake.

As Chico leaped to slam the ball into the goal's net, the crowd stood their feet with a cheer and applaud so loud that it could make a deaf person hear. The team had reclaimed victory as they hugged and pushed each other.

Derek jumped up and down as Coach Myers slapped the other teammates on their back. It was a night of defeat and one of the best nights in the history of the Carolina Stingers.

Derek couldn't be happier for his hard work towards coaching the team and leading them to win, but deep down he was filled with hurt and confusion as he thought of Lia.

He wished that she could have been there rooting in the audience, but she wasn't. Instead she was at home in bed (or so she claimed.) because of her injured foot. The same injured foot that she switched up on. Derek was going to get to put the puzzle pieces together once and for all, he just needed time.

***

"It's good to see your foot is getting better, baby." Derek said to Lia as they were sitting on the couch one evening watching television.

Lia looked over across at Derek as the light from the television glistened on her beautiful brown face. "Thanks, I've been trying to put pressure on it so it could heal faster."

Derek shook his head as he reached for the bowl of popcorn. "You know you're supposed to be taking it easy. I want you to let Calvin take a look at it tomorrow when I take you to his office. He'll tell you what medication you need."

"I don't need your brother to be my doctor. I'm doing just fine healing on my own." She pouted, running her hand through her thick hair as if she were tying it with an imaginary hairband.

Derek absolutely loved it whenever she played in her hair like that. It drove him crazy like a mad man.

He reached over to smooth his hands over her thick thighs. She wore short pajamas that revealed the juiciness of her thighs. Derek slapped her playfully on the thigh and bit his bottom lip. "Do you know how much I love you?"

Lia rolled her eyes. "No, how much?"

Leaning over to kiss her on the neck, Derek pulled her in closer to him. "This much."

She moaned as she slowly wrapped her arm around his neck. "Mmm. I guess you've finally gotten over your insecurity rampage, huh?"

Derek snuggled and smacked his lips on her neck. "I'm just trying not to let anything regarding assumptions interrupt us when we're almost down the aisle. As my mother would say, the devil stirs up trouble where they ain't trouble."

"Mmm. I am loving the sound of that. See, baby. It was all in your head. It all started with me being very busy at work which started you to feel insecure. What made it worse was that I called you Denzel during sex just because you resembled Denzel Washington. You thought it seemed fishy because one of the athletes on your team's middle name is Denzel and you took it out on him, poor kid."

"Yeah, I guess I owe him an apology." Derek laughed through a mouthful of their kisses. "You know; it was probably him that called my cell phone to prank me with the sounds of a woman having sex."

Lia leaned her head back to find his face. "Yes, that could always be true. I told you that could be a reason."

"Well, I don't care anymore. It's all over with now and it was just a misunderstanding. I'm just ready to make you Mrs. Derek Belin and I'm ready to fill this house up with little Derek Belins running around." He laughed.

"Ohhh, well let's get started now. We have a lot of making up to do." Lia said sexily with a purr in her voice.

Derek kissed her slowly, allowing her body to lay back into the sofa. As they were making out on the couch like two teenagers on the low, Derek felt something sticking out from under the pillow.

"Mmmm what is it, baby? Why did you stop?" asked a confused Lia.

"I feel something hard sticking me." He said as he tried to sit up in an upright position on the sofa.

Lia groaned. "It's probably just my nipples you feel against you. They do happen to get hard like diamonds."

As enticing as Lia sounded and as bad as Derek wanted to make love to her again, he had to see what the metal object was that had stuck him on the shoulder.

Derek fished his hands around and under the side of the pillow and pulled out a watch. A watch that didn't belong to him or Lia. It was a large Rolex watch with diamonds so big it could make a blind man see. It sure as hell wasn't his.

Lia gasped as if she had seen a ghost. She brought two hands up to her face to cover up the verbal evidence that would escape from her mouth.

Reaching to turn on the lamp that sat on the end table beside the plush sofa, Derek kept his eyes glued angrily on Lia. He examined the Rolex watch;

holding it up in the air as though he was investigating an object from a crime scene like Ice T did on *Law and Order.*

"Derek shook his head slowly. The frown on his forehead was cut so deep that his veins concealed through his pecan complexion. "Who does this watch belong to, Lia?"

Lia jumped and squealed like a little girl.

Her hands shook like a cocaine addict in need of some good stuff.

"FUCKIN ANSWER ME, LIA! YOU'VE GOT TOO MANY EXCUSES NOW, WOMAN!"

"Derek I—I don't know how that got here?"

"STOP LYING TO ME, LIA! WHO THE FUCK IS **M.B**, HUH? Whose initials are engraved on this watch? My initials sure aren't **M.B**!" Derek threw the watch at her.

There was still silence as Lia wiped away her tears. She had no explanation. She had nothing to say because she was busted. She stared at him frozen like a deer in headlights.

Derek walked over to her and pulled her by the wrist like an unruly child. "Go get your shit and get the fuck out of my house right now! You're a lying and a cheating ass! Why would you let this take place in my house though, Lia? The house that I am paying for with my own damn money. Why would you bring another man in my house to cheat on me with? Why would you fuck up just a few days before the wedding? WHY?!"

"Derek, where am I supposed to go? You can't just put me out on the street?" was all Lia could say as she threw her hands around.

She actually had the audacity to bring up the concern of where she would stay and not about his feelings. Derek knew right then and there that her feelings for him were no longer there. She had been a stranger in his house who had even invited a stranger in his house while he was gone.

Derek placed both his hands on his hips as he looked down at the floor and took a deep breath. He was tired. "Lia, just get out of my house right now. I don't want to see your face. I don't want to hear your voice. I don't want to smell the scent of your perfume or the scent of another man on your body. You're disgusting! You're just like Eve in the bible! You're just like Delilah when she betrayed Samson! A woman just can't be trusted!"

Lia tried to wrap her arms around his neck, but he pushed her away with a strong force that caused her to fall to the floor. She looked up at him in disbelief. She gave him a deep stare as she realized she had seen another side to him and it was a side that she created.

Derek knew that it must be true since she had nothing else to say based on her will to comfort him. He just wanted her far away from him as possible.

"Put your clothes on and just leave. I'll have all of your belongings sent over to your parents' house by tomorrow." Derek replied, rubbing his head from the headache. His nerves were everywhere as he anxiously tapped his foot.

She could not look into his eyes; she was too ashamed to. She picked up her jeans and slowly placed them over her mountainous hips, grabbing her purse. "I'll just get in my car and get out of here. I don't know what I am going to tell my family. They're all expecting the wedding to take place any time now. I can't stay with them. You know they live in the hood."

At one point, Derek wanted to laugh, but he couldn't. Lia was just too much of a character and her true colors were coming out into the light and showing. Derek pointed towards the door, signaling for her to leave and get the hell out of his life.

When she walked away slowly and shut the door behind her, Derek leaned his back against the door with his hand over his chest. He felt like someone had ran over his heart with a Mack truck, crushing it and every bit of it left.

Chapter 10

A walk at the park had been nice, but Derek's engagement to Lia was no longer a walk in the park. He was most definitely a mama's boy and that was why he had invited his mother with him to Columbia Community Park. She was the first one that he told everything to and he would rather let her be the first before anyone else. At first Shirley was startled when he told her, but she wasn't concerned for long.

"Baby, sometimes you have to go through thousands of women before you find the right one." Shirley said, patting her son on the back.

Derek took a long sigh as he shook his head. "I know, mama. But I don't want to go through that many women. I mean, I'm ready to get married and start a family. Well, at least I was ready to get started and start a family. I'm not even sure if I feel like I can trust anyone now. She was cheating on me. The evidence was already there before I even noticed physical evidence. Mother, she was calling another man's name while we were making love and she was working long hours. What photographer do you know works that late and misses out on dinner more than two times in a week?"

"Derek, just know that what goes around comes back around. God is the judge in the end and that is one saying that makes me believe that He is the one in control." Shirley lectured. "You just can't blame every woman for one woman's mistakes."

A cool wind was coming their way, causing the trees to dance and the South Carolina flag to make a whipping sound from a nearby pole. Derek had to admit that he felt at ease whenever he had a conversation with his mother. She understood him more than anyone and in fact, he always felt that he was the favorite son out of the family.

"Mother, has dad ever had an affair?" he asked.

Shirley was caught off guard as she gasped.

"I'm sorry, mother. I just…had to ask. I guess I want to know if you know what it feels like. If so, what did you do and how did you handle it? You know I always come to you for everything." Derek said, searching for hope on his mother's face.

She smiled as she stopped walking to look her son in his big, beautiful brown eyes. "It's okay, baby. I don't mind you asking that at all. We may have to sit here on the nearby bench because I have a story to tell you."

Derek helped to escort his mother to the bench by wrapping his arm around her shoulder. It had brought back childhood memories when he and his mother would take walks in the park while his brothers all went fishing with their late father.

Derek never really cared much for fishing like his other brothers. They always took after their father with a passion for fishing and doing things agricultural.

"Mother, this makes me think of the time you would take me to play ball in the park while Montez, Calvin, Malik and Devontae went on fishing trips with father. Do you remember that?" he asked, sitting on the bench. A few hikers jogged by them and a woman arguing on her cell phone was power walking in the distance.

Shirley was looking at the ducks as she laughed at the memory. "Of course I remember that. I'm not that old to remember, son. They all took after your father with that part, but you didn't. You took after me"

Derek looked up at the sky at the soaring grey clouds. It would probably start raining anytime soon.

"Son, your father did cheat on me. It only happened once. I tried to hide the fact that he did and I got over it, but I will never forget what the pain was like." Shirley confessed.

A bomb dropped in the pit of Derek's stomach as he repeated in his mind what his mother had just told him.

Derek's face was now red. "Mother, you aren't serious, are you?" he gulped nervously. "Mother, I can't take any more than I can bare."

"You ASKED if your dad has ever had an affair, but he wouldn't be able to tell you that because he's dead." She slowly searched through her purse for a napkin and began to wipe the tears from the corners of her eyes. "I had an affair with someone after discovering that he had an affair."

Derek rose from his seat. "So daddy had an affair? You both had an affair? It seems so hard to believe and you both covered it well."

Shirley sniffled. "Yes, son. That is true."

"But, mother-"

"I had an affair because my heart was breaking when I noticed him cheating on me with a woman on the church choir, my best friend. You know how friendly your father was with everyone and always praying for them and doing the Lord's work. He was a little too God-given." She interrupted.

Derek anxiously stroked the hair around his face with trembling hands. "Oh, mother! You must have been hurt, he must have been hurt! You both hurt each other! Being hurt is not supposed to be a part of marriage! You both seemed so happy! How did you cope with him cheating? What did you do?

I can't take any of this! It's too much for me! I'm going crazy!"

Derek's loud outburst had caused the pigeons on a nearby building to fly away with the wind and the speed of sound.

"Son, marriage is no easy process. Your father never knew I discovered his affair and he never discovered about mine. The bible says that we are supposed to work through the marriage and be there through sickness and in health." Shirley cried.

"Yes, mother! The bible sure as hell didn't say to commit adultery! If marriage is this dramatic then I don't know if I want any part of it." Derek took a seat again, shaking his head.

Shirley pulled him in closer for him to rest his head on her shoulder. She stroked his wavy hair just like when he was a little boy. "You can't let your brothers know any of this. It will only bring things down and confuse everything. I wanted everyone to stay happy. I wanted to keep my family together. I got over the pain of a man I loved by getting under another man. I regretted my sin and I asked God for forgiveness. I don't know how your father felt after his affair, but I know he must have felt remorseful because he kept buying me gifts and constantly telling me how much he loved me. The guilt was torture for him."

"So you're trying to tell me that Lia is going to feel her conscience torturing her cheating on me?" Derek sat up to look his mother in her eyes. "Mother, that doesn't do anything for me. I don't know what to do."

Not knowing what else to tell Derek, the only thing Shirley could do was to embrace him into her arms. Of course she had to stand on her tippy toes just because he was a little over six feet, but he made sure he bent down just so she could reach him.

"Derek, I don't want you to lose yourself over this. I want you to keep on being successful and keep on being you. If you still love Lia and if she loves you, maybe you both can work it out. Love can beat anything. It's the strongest power we humans have. My love was so strong for your father that I fought through it and I forgave him, I also forgave myself. Time heals all. Allow your wound to heal and develop a new shed of skin. A shed of skin that is stronger and solid. That's what I did. That's the answer I have for you, son and I hope it helps." Shirley preached.

Smiling at his mother, Derek had never felt so much comfort in his life. Shirley always gave him that warm feeling and he wouldn't know what he would do without her in his life. Nodding his head, Derek had come to a realization. "Mother, you have helped me more than you will ever know." He kissed her on the cheek.

Shirley was surprised as a smirk grew on her face. "Oh? So what is it that you are going to do?"

"I'm going to give myself a little time to heal and get over this. So many happily married couples who have been together for years have cheated on each other and reconciled stronger while in their marriage. No one ever suspects it. What matters is how strong two people work together to keep their glue bonded. In marriage, if you love someone you can't just walk away without even trying. You will hurt, but you must try to forgive, forget and build more stable walls." Derek explained with a little more confidence in his tone than before.

Shirley laughed. "That's right!"

Derek leaned in to kiss her on the cheek once more. "I love you, mother."

"I love you too, son. Now let's call our driver and get out of here before it rains. I just left the salon earlier and I wouldn't want to mess up for my new curls." She said, patting her hair into a place. She recently had it dyed a little darker, but the few strands of grey still peeked through.

As they walked along, Derek bent his arm so that Shirley could slide her arm through.

He could see the pain in his mother's eyes and hear it in her voice. He hugged her long and hard as she released her tears. "No need to go through that pain again, mother. I can understand why you did the things you did. Being hurt by a loved one is one of the most painful feelings in the world. No matter how much pain you were in, you forgave him and you forgave yourself. You also worked through it and strengthened your marriage with him. Mother, that is exactly what I should do with Lia. I have found my answer. It's just going to take a little more healing."

The mascara around Shirley's eyes were smeared as she gave a weak laugh. "Good. That's good. I'm glad you are going to work through it and give it another shot. Love is too strong to walk away from sometimes, especially if it was based on a good history."

The two of them made their way to the driver as he opened the door to the 2016 Aston Martin. Derek held his mother's hand as they rode together in the back seat. He had a lot of discovery to do. He decided that he was going to try and reconcile with Lia.

Reconciling with Lia would be hard, but she would have to be willing to make a few changes for them to grow together.

Chapter 11

Staying at her parent's place in the projects was the last place where Lia would want to go. Luckily, she had a few bucks saved up in the bank from her paycheck from work. All of the credit cards that Derek had gave her where back at his house. Shit. How could she have ruined a good thing?!

Lia looked up at the average style hotel known as Palmetto Inn. If she had had one of the credit cards that Derek shared with her then she could have been staying at one of the fancier hotels. Unfortunately, she had to do what she had to do until things got better.

As she walked into the hotel lobby, she noticed a few low-lives standing around the vending machine. She kept her head down underneath a Georgia Bulldogs baseball cap, she didn't want to risk anyone she knew spotting her in some cheap hotel.

The receptionist at the front desk looked up at her as she filed her nails and chewed her bubble gum. "How may I help you?"

"Yes, I'd like a single smoking room, please." Lia said nervously.

The receptionist blew a loud bubble before responding. "I'm gonna need to see some I.D first."

Lia rushed her hands through her black leather Michael Kors purse and pulled out her driver's license. She slapped it down on the desk and looked around, observing the scene.

"Girl, you seem like you're in a hurry! Are you running from the FBI or some shit?" the receptionist laughed, still smacking on her bubble gum. "That's a nice engagement ring you're wearing by the way. The designer bag is looking flashy too, damn. What's a well-to do lady like yourself checking into this hotel when you could have gone over to Grand Central Suite?"

Lia rolled her eyes, wishing that the nosy receptionist wouldn't ask her anymore questions. "Look, I just need to get a room and I need to get it now! It's not your job to ask why I'm staying deciding to check in here or not! Just be thankful that I'm paying you money to get your ghetto nails and weave done!!"

Oh, she had really pissed the receptionist off now. She had some nerve to try her like that. The receptionist raised an eyebrow and pursed her lips as hard as she could to prepare for what she was about to say. "Look here, you high maintenance snobby rich bitch! You don't have to get a damn attitude with me like that acting like you're the bitch that runs the place! You can't even check in any damn way!"

The bystanders in the lobby were clapping their hands and laughing at what they were witnessing, a few of them must have been alcoholics because Lia could smell them from a distance.

"Well why the hell can't I check in? I hope you don't think that this place is too good for me. I'm just trying to be smart and save some money at the moment; something some people probably should learn how to do." Lia snapped, staring the receptionist up and down as she noticed the bee-hive of a hairdo she wore on her head. Straight out of the hood.

The receptionist threw Lia's license across the desk at her. She had totally caught Lia off guard. "Your damn license is expired anyway. Get the fuck out of her, trick."

Lia shook her head as she picked up her license. She bawled her fist tightly into the palm of her hand as she gave an angry frown at the receptionist.

A part of her wanted to let the true hidden ghetto girl out and get into a cat fight, but she knew that would be uncalled for. Instead she stormed out the lobby as the bells on the door dangled loudly.

She didn't have to take this from a hood rat or anyone else.

When Lia made it outside in the parking lot, she leaned against her car and pulled out her cell phone. She was tempted to call Derek and ask him to forgive her. She really wanted to just slap herself and knock some sense into her head.

She loved Derek deep down with all her heart. There was no one else she wanted to be with other than him. He was the world's most perfect man. He had everything. He had charming good looks, he was well-educated with a good career and came from a rich family.

If he was so perfect, then why in the hell did she cheat on him with another man? That was something she couldn't answer her damn self.

She opened the door to her car and took a seat behind the wheel. She removed her hat and rested her head against the wall.

Thoughts of the other man had appeared in her mind. He had something that Derek lacked and Derek had something that he needed.

This other man simply made Lia feel free. He didn't bombard her with a lot of questions or made her feel trapped. He allowed her to express her feminism both mentally and physically, unlike Derek who tried to be controlling and old fashioned. Sexually, Derek liked to take control, but there were times that Lia wanted to be the one in control. The sex between them was good as hell, but she still like to take over and do things her way.

The only way she could be free sexually was when she was with the other man. The other man never haunted her down or made her feel like she had to behave a certain way just because he was from a perfect family.

Lia wanted so badly to combine both Derek and the other man and create them into one man, but she knew she that would be impossible. She couldn't have her cake and eat it too. She did have feelings for the other man, but only wish he was as supportive and caring as Derek.

She glided her French manicured fingertips over the cellular phone with tears falling from her mahogany colored eyes. The busy sound of traffic played from afar as little specks of rain began tapping on the roof of her car.

There was only one person she could call to take her in and as guilty as she felt reaching out to him, she had no other choice.

"Hello?" he answered.

"He found out. He found out about us and I have no way to go. May I come stay with you until I figure out what to do?" she cried.

Chapter 12

He met her at a nearby coffee shop that didn't have that much of a crowd. The two of them sat at the farthest end of the shop and shared a mocha latte in a cozy little booth beside the wall. The blond haired waitress kept refilling their cups in what seemed like every five minutes.

"So it's completely over between you two? No engagement? No upcoming wedding? How did he find out about us? Does he know about me?" The other man asked anxiously, taking a sip from his hot latte. The steam was rising above his lips, warning him that it was too hot to drink normally. He placed the cup down gently as he studied Lia's eyes.

"No." Lia began, tapping her fingers along the table. "He doesn't know about you, but he found your watch in the sofa while we were making out. After he discovered that, he threw me out and started cussing like a sailor. He was hurt and I don't blame him."

The other man gasped. "You were making out with him? I thought you said that sex between you two was like two old zombies trying to raise from the dead?"

Lia rolled her eyes. "Have you forgot that I lived with him? Of course we made out. I'm not going to lie to you."

He looked around as though he was being watched; feeling his palms sweat and it wasn't from firmly holding the cup of latte.

"I need some where to stay. I need to stay with you for a little while JUST until I get some place of my own. You know I have always depended on Derek for everything, even though I have a job. But with my job alone it's not as much as I had with Derek's help." Lia licked her lips.

"Well, I'm just glad he didn't find out it was me you're cheating with. Do you know what that would do between me and him?" The other man took a deep breath, still looking around and over his shoulder. He jumped every time he heard someone coming in through the door.

Slapping her hands on the table top, Lia demanded for his attention. "Look, aren't you even listening to what I'm saying? I need a fuckin place to stay! Can I crash with you or not?"

The other man leaned in a little closer just so Lia could whiff the scent of his foreign cologne. "Sure, baby. I'll let you stay with me. You can stay with me for as long as you like. You know that I want to be with you. I've always wanted to, regardless of Derek thinks."

"I know. I want to be with you too, but this wasn't right. It has to end. I'm just asking for a place to stay or at least a paid room in a nice hotel.

Please!" Lia said with a desperate urge on her face. She was almost in tears and that gave the other man power somehow.

"Baby." He reached across the table to place her small hands into the palm of his buttery brown hands. "We can still continue to keep our relationship going. He doesn't have to know. As long as you're in my life then what harm is it that we love each other secretly?"

He was just making this even more hard on her. Didn't he understand that she was under a lot of pressure? Obviously, he was selfish and this was one of the reasons why she couldn't be with him fully.

"That's just it right there! I don't want to live a secret love life. That is no way to be happy. I will be feeling guilt and I will also be feeling ashamed if he were to ever see us to together. My conscience would kill me! Don't you get it? No more of this!" cried Lia. She was feeling devastated as she rested her head in the palm of her hand.

The other man smiled. "Well, if this is going to be the end and if you want me to help you out with a place to stay, then you have to do me a favor this one last time, Lia."

Lia looked up at him with tear filled eyes. At that point she was desperate for a warm place to stay, just for tonight. "What's that?" she asked.

He looked up at her with a wink as if she could read his mind in regards to the favor.

Chapter 13

The rain poured over them as they rushed anxiously towards the front door of his fancy imperial mansion.

Angel statues greeted them at the end of the two bannisters of what seemed liked it catered a thousand stairs. The marbled style floors glistened underneath the exquisite chandeliers that hung above them. Crimson colored Arabian drapes accented the large ceiling to floor windows that granted them the privacy that they needed.

The "other" man kissed her seductively, allowing his tongue to dance with hers in a romantic rhythm.

He knew her body, he knew her body completely as he removed her sweatshirt to reveal her luscious breasts peering through the cup of her laced bra.

He picked her up and carried her up the exaggerated stairs, cradling her legs around his masculine waist as he drunk her many kisses.

He slammed her against the wall once they made it to the bedroom as he kissed trails all over body. Sucking her lips, her neck, her belly button and madly removing her sweatpants to bury his face in her sweet spot. Lia racked her fingers through his hair to guide his movements inside of her.

"Oh, your mouth feels so good. Your tongue feels so good inside of me. Mmmmm." Lia moaned.

He groaned like a lion, cupping her buttocks as he pulled her into his face. He smelled her feminine juices as they left a stain in the follicles of his facial hair. He wasn't done yet.

The other man carried her to the king size bed and placed her down gently. He shook his head as his brown eyes focused on her. He was watching her every move like she was his trapped prey.

The other man removed his wet shirt to reveal his chiseled muscles and what seemed to be a six pack. He was tight and ripped, maybe a little more ripped than Derek.

"This is what you'll be missing, Lia." He told her as he climbed over her. "How do you want it?"

Lia loved that he was both submissive and demanding all in one. With Derek, he would always take it and do what he wanted without letting her have her way as much. With the other man, he took charge and also offered what she desired to do.

"Mmmm I want it from the back. I want you to take me from behind." Lia bit her bottom lip, staring deeply and madly into his eyes.

The sound of rain started to pour harder on the roof top.

The other man offered her a sly smile as he gently turned her over until she was on all-fours. He rubbed her ass before he prepared to give it a rough smack. "That's just pretty." He said, referring to gravity of her mountainous ass.

He reached over to his night stand to grab a latex condom. Sheep's skin was always best skin to use. It made the friction between her legs feel oh-the more real.

He placed the package between his teeth as he removed it from the foil and then slid it over his large member that was already dripping with his pre-ejaculate. He was more than ready and he was ready to tear her up like a wolf.

Spreading her ass cheeks apart and hearing the sound of her wetness, Lia moaned and purred like a cat.

Her body trembled, remembering how Derek was never as good as the other man. She wanted him and she wanted him all the time, but that was impossible. She made sure she enjoyed him just one last time.

He slid through her tight walls as he made a hissing sound, almost like a snack. At that moment he was about to explode because she felt so amazing, but he remained manly and strong. He gripped the softness of her ass as he splashed and forced his large member inside of her.

Lia tried to rock her weight back into him, but he was just too full. He was much too long as she felt him crawling through her pelvis and up her stomach. Lia couldn't call on anyone else but God as he picked up his pace, rocking himself inside of her.

"Shit, you have some good pussy, woman! Holy fuck!" He screamed, adding a slap to her ass.

"Awwww yeah! Give it to me one last time. Make it last forever, baby!" She licked her lips, dipping her head back.

The other man wasn't playing any games, reminding her of why she cheated on Derek in the first place.

"You sure you want to end this, Lia? Huh? Answer me!" The other man whispered in her ears, causing her vaginal lips to tighten around him. The way his sexy voices sound had made her nerves lose control.

The king size bed was squeaking at its loudest. It would probably break if they continued making love like psychopathic rabbits, but they didn't care.

The room was filled with their screams and moans. The scent of their sweat and sex had created the perfect smelling fragrance created by nature.

When it was all over, they both collapse on top of each other. The other man allowed his body weight to cover Lia as they were both out of breath. They panted like two runners making it to the finish line and claiming their victory.

Chapter 14

Derek smiled as he ran his hands over his head as he looked at the cracked photo of he and Lia. *She cheated on me, okay. Big deal. At least she did it before we took vows. I can get over this..*he thought to himself.

He could hear his brother Malik telling him to be careful and guard his heart. He and Malik may not agree eye to eye on things, but his brother always knew what to do in times like these. As a matter of fact, he needed to talk with him before he gave Lia a second chance. He really needed his brother's input.

Grabbing a light jacket from the coat rack, Derek wasn't about to waste any time. He was going to drive over to Malik's place immediately to have a late night chat with him.

Malik always told him that if he needed to chat about it that he could contact him day or night. He knew that Malik was always up late going over court trial notes for upcoming cases, sometimes he was up until four o'clock in the morning preparing.

As Derek pulled out of his garage in one of his Camaros, he was already feeling confident about turning over a new leaf. He knew he lost his cool when he discovered that Lia was cheating, but he was willing to put it all behind him. If it hadn't been for his mother sharing with him strength she and his father had during his infidelity, he wouldn't be sure if he would consider letting the wedding go on…if it wasn't too late.

Derek thought of ways he was going to reconcile with Lia as he drove under the dark sky of highway I-95. Luther Vandross was singing his popular hit *Here and Now* on the radio and Derek started to sing along.

Finally, he made it to Malik's home and realized that all the lights were out except for one light that was upstairs on the third floor. Derek smiled as he had an image of his brother practicing on how to show off in court. Malik would always pace back and forth, rubbing his chin whenever he trying to put together a case.

Derek laughed in the car as he looked up at the window, remembering how when they were kids that Malik would put on an act as a lawyer.

He got out of the car and quietly shut his door behind him. When he arrived at Malik's front door he was about to knock, but decided he wouldn't. He knew that Malik had a spare key under the rug so he used that to sneak in and give him a scare. Derek laughed like a rotten little boy as he used the key to open the door.

Once he made it inside the dark home, he crept up the stairs quietly. It was a good thing that the bright moon was shining through the windows to give him the light that he needed. Derek tried his best not to laugh as he pictured Malik being scared shitless. He chuckled while he held on to the bannister and walked up the stairs. Just a few more steps and he was near the bedroom.

He got closer and closer. Something didn't sound right. Something sounded too familiar. Derek's smile transformed into an angry frown as his heart dropped to the pit of his stomach.

Malik's bedroom door was completely open as he saw what he thought his eyes were playing tricks on him. He thought he was seeing double vision. He wasn't sure if he was dreaming or not. If he was dreaming, then it sure was one of the worst nightmares ever.

Derek saw Malik and then he saw Lia being pounded and man handled by him. Both of them moaning, creating a symphony that felt sweet to their ears, but was heart wrenching to Derek's. It was then that he realized the man Lia was cheating with behind his back was his own brother. His own flesh and blood.

Chapter 15

Derek wasted no time in pulling Malik by the neck so that he could get a good angle to punch him in the face. Lia's naked body leaped from the bed as she screamed in the corner.

Malik's head dipped back with a harsh force as Derek gave him punch after punch and blow after blow. Derek was going completely mad and his mind was completely lost at that moment. All he saw was red and all he felt was intense anger.

His fist was covered in blood, not just Malik's blood, but his own blood. The way he was graphically giving his brother the beat down was just too much.

"Derek! Derek! I-" Malik couldn't get a word in as he begged and pleaded. He couldn't fight back for the fact that was completely naked and caught off guard.

Derek slammed him against the wall and threw him to the floor like a rag doll, curb kicking him in the pit of his stomach. The only thing Malik could do was guard his face and scream for his life. His older brother was much stronger than him.

"How in the hell could you do this to me, man? You are my brother!!!" Derek yelled as he looked down at a blood coughing Malik.

Malik raised his hands to surrender for Derek to stop. "Derek, I'm so sorry, man! I made a stupid MISTAKE! A real stupid mistake!!!"

Lia tried to step in, walking up to Derek in fear of him being out of control and using his violence on her. "Derek…I'm so sorry, baby! I… I was scared! I was confused! I was stressed! I….."

Tears stained Derek's face as he looked at Lia. She could no longer look him in the eyes for she was too embarrassed. "With my own brother, Lia? What the fuck is wrong with you? What the fuck is wrong with both of you? I loved you and was willing to make this work had it been with somebody else. But for you to cheat behind my back with my brother! My own brother! This has got to be the craziest shit ever!"

Lia cried as she covered her trembling hands over her mouth. Her cries sounded like a mourning widower at a dreadful funeral, both chilling and sadistic.

Derek shook his head in disbelief. He looked down at Malik who was curled up in a fetal position, naked, cold and embarrassed.

"I will never see you two the same as I did before." He kept his eyes fixed on Malik. "I guess you're the serpent that finally turned into a snake, huh brother? Look at the way you are on the floor just lying there. You should be able to crawl on your stomach for the rest of your life!"

"Baby, please This is totally not the-" Lia tried to comfort Derek.

Derek pushed her hand away from him quickly. "Don't touch me, Eve! Maybe God named Eve that name because he knew that she would be evil! You're evil! You're an evil woman, Lia!"

Lia still continued to plead for his forgiveness, but he pushed her down to the floor beside his injured brother who was nearly unconscious.

Derek took his time to leave their presence. He walked away slowly and out of the home towards his car where he cried for a half an hour before pulling out the drive way.

Before putting the car in drive and leaving , he rested his head on the steering wheel and poured his heart out like he did when his father died. He had never felt that amount of pain in his life and thought that it wouldn't repeat itself again.

Derek felt the burning sensation throughout his heart, his veins and in his blood. Having a broken heart was something hard to live with, more than the feeling of physical pain to him.

Chapter 16

It had been days since Derek left him home. The mansion was completely silent and most of the time Derek stayed in his bed to stare of at the ceiling above him, wearing the same pajamas he had worn almost all week.

He had glanced over at a text message from his brother Calvin, telling him to get out of bed and wash his ass. He powered the phone off and slept the morning away.

It wasn't until later that evening when his mother called and left a tearful message on the voicemail of his home phone.

"Baby, I am just calling to check on you. You are always in my heart and I love you and all of your brothers. I know how you feel, trust me. That feeling is not a good feeling, but it is one that can be defeated with time. I just want this family to be a family again. Blood is thicker than water, no matter what. You have to pull yourself together and do what I did in order to get through. I love you, son."

Derek wiped away tears as he sat up on the side of his bed. The clock beside his night stand said that it was 6:00pm. Derek knew he had lost a good bit of weight and he eventually he had to get back on his feet. He had blocked all calls from Lia and even had her removed from his joint bank account. Word on the street was that she was out of work and living in the projects with her parents again until she found a way out.

Derek wanted nothing but karma to be restored upon her. Deep down inside, Derek still loved Malik. He knew he could never stay upset at him forever.

It was very similar to a situation in high school were Malik had stolen Derek's girlfriend, except back then it wasn't with his fiancé. The two of them patched things up after beating the bricks off of one another.

Derek took a long breath as he agreed on what he was about to do next. It was going to be a tough decision. After he took a shower and cleaned himself up, he was going to go over to his mother's mansion for dinner and reconcile with his brother during their traditional family dinner.

After he stepped out of the shower heading towards his bathroom for a shower, he heard a rattling sound from outside. The sound was the similar one he had been hearing in his home for the past few weeks.

Derek gently patted his pecan tanned complexion with a decorative towel that was neatly folded on the towel shelf. He quietly dried his entire masculine body before covering himself in a blue terry cloth bathrobe.

"Hello?" he called out, walking down the hallway towards his backdoor.

The sound was coming from the garage. Someone was tampering with his garage door and trying to get in. Derek gulped, feeling his blood beginning to boil from his nerves. Who could this mysterious intruder be that tried to enter his home?

As Derek stepped out the backdoor, he was in shock as he noticed the burglar hunched over his Camaro trying to unlock it with a clothes hanger. What caught his attention was that the burglar's body was very feminine in the all black body suit. She was curvaceous in size and her hips were well proportioned.

Derek snuck behind her so close that she could smell the scent of his body wash. Derek tightened his large hands around her mouth so that she wouldn't be able to scream.

"Don't scream…or you'll be sorry." He whispered.

The beautiful burglar was caught off guard. She thought that she would be the one to escape away easy, but things had turned around the opposite way.

This robbery was going to be a little different, especially since Derek was feeling vulnerable at the moment and he was just getting over the most excruciating pain in his life.

"You want to steal something from me, I'm going to steal something valuable from you." He said in a sexy and devilish tone. "Stand still and don't move."

The sexy burglar stood frozen as Derek made his way to the glove compartment of his car. What he was searching for was a condom. He always kept them with him everywhere.

Once Derek had received the condom, he dropped his bathrobe to reveal his naked body right there in his garage. He turned the burglar around so that she could face him.

He would have had her get on his knees to proceed with her punishment, but he was too much of a gentleman. Instead he ripped off her black top to notice her perky breasts. She wasn't wearing a bra, but the cold night air had them standing up at attention just right.

She was about to speak, but he placed his finger over her lips. "Don't say a word." He told her. "It's better this way."

Derek licked his lips as he eyed her body up and down. He was tempted to remove the black burglar mask she wore. All he could see was her eyes peering through the hole and her the curve of her thick lips. Her eyes looked so familiar, so deep and romantic. He decided to let her keep the mask on because it would make things more intriguing.

Removing her black tights, Derek also noticed that she wore no panties. "Mmmmm." He moaned. "I'm gonna make you pay for your crime right now."

The burglar took the initiative to spread her legs apart so that Derek could take a look her at her below. Somehow she was turned on by it as well.

Derek pushed her against the car madly as he made angry sex to her. The sex he gave her allowed him to work out his frustration over Lia. The burglar's moans sounded painful as she took him in.

Derek chocked her as he pumped her with every force and inch that she could take. He groaned with temper and outrage while he choked her neck even more.

The sex seemed more like a violent rape, but one that was filled with passion on Derek's in. Her juices soaked around him as he pinned her against his car with her legs around his waist. Derek grunted, feeling himself let out a passionate outrage.

When he was done, he was lethargic and satisfied. "That will teach you to burglarize my car. Don't ever let it happen again."

Shockingly, the burglar removed her mask as she shook her long hair into place. "Don't worry, Derek. I'll make sure that it won't."

Derek's mouth nearly dropped to the ground when he realized that the burglar was none other...than Lia.

<u>CAN'T GET ENOUGH OF THE BELIN BROTHERS?</u>

If you enjoyed reading *The Belin Brothers: A Stranger in My House,* then you should read his brother Calvin's story. *The Belin Brothers: A Stranger's Desire.* It can be purchased via paperback and by searching through Amazon

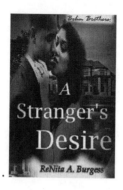

Kindle readers click go here:
https://www.amazon.com/Strangers-Desire-Belin-Brothers-ebook/dp/B01EZF84WQ?ie=UTF8&ref_=zg_bs_1 0159287011_42

*Be kind and leave a review. ☺ I always love hearing from my readers and enjoyed having you as my audience. God bless!

*Also, book 3 in the series will be available **2017**. STAY TUNED!*

ABOUT *THE AUTHOR*

ReNita A. Burgess is a two-time Amazon best-selling author who refers to herself as a classy southern belle, but whenever she writes she can become anyone she wants. Writing has always been a passion and a talent of hers ever since she was a young girl.

Today she has published 30 books of different genres; horror, romance, inspiration, children's, suspense... you name it. ReNita has been on both television and radio interviews regarding her collection of books.

ReNita discovered her passion for writing at the age of 8 years old while sitting at the back of the class. Her teacher noticed she wasn't looking at the board because she was too busy writing imaginative stories. When the teacher was about to argue with ReNita for not paying attention to the lesson, she was impressed as she read ReNita's stories. The teacher's encouragement prompted ReNita to hold on to her dream of becoming an author someday.

When ReNita isn't busy typing away until her fingers are sore, she's either working out, watching Lifetime or shopping. She lives in South Carolina with her spoiled Chihuahua/Jack Russell.

Made in the USA
Middletown, DE
15 May 2023

30604294R00078